MW00523211

You
ROCK
My
World

Edited by SUSAN DAVIS

Illustrated by MARY ROSS

you

ROCK

my

WORLD

!!!

The Crazy Little Book of Love

Ariel Books

**Andrews McMeel
Publishing**

Kansas City

Illustrations © 2001 by Mary Ross

ISBN: 0-7407-1964-5
Library of Congress Catalog Card Number: 2001087918

Contents

Introduction   7

Head Over Heels   11

Crazy Love   25

The Joys of Misery   41

Throwing Caution to the Wind   55

You Rock My World   65

Introduction

L ove has been called a whirlwind, a torrent, a fire, and a sweet madness. It sweeps you off your feet, rages through you like a river in flood, sets your heart ablaze, and leaves you either speechless or babbling deliriously.

Love rocks your world.

Love can neither be tamed nor contained. It knows no boundaries and won't shy from delicious and dangerous pursuits. It swallows you whole and carries you along downstream through a magical, uncertain landscape: past fields of brilliant flowers,

you ROCK my *World*

past glades and tangled thickets, through raging
rapids and calmer waters.

Love rocks your world.

When love finds you—whether it's first love, true
love, or one-and-only love—one thing is certain:

You are changed forever.

Head Over Heels

Love is a fire. But whether it is going to warm your hearth or burn down your house, you can never tell.

—Joan Crawford

Falling in love is not an extension of one's limits or boundaries; it is a partial and temporary collapse of them.

—M. Scott Peck

The sweetest joy, the wildest woe is love.

—Pearl Bailey

Lolita, light of my life, fire of my loins. My sin,
my soul.

—Vladimir Nabokov, *Lolita*

She felt she had been pitched from a safe, calm har-
bor into an unpredictable and turbulent sea; that
she had woken up not from a dream but from a day-
dream. Falling in love opened the world up to her in
a way it had not been opened before.

—Laurie Colwin, *Family Happiness*

To fall in love you have to be in a state of mind for
it to take, like a disease.

—Nancy Mitford

Never forget that the most powerful force
on earth is love.

—Nelson Rockefeller

If it is your time love will track you down like a cruise missile. If you say "No! I don't want it right now," that's when you'll get it for sure. Love will make a way out of no way. Love is an exploding cigar which we willingly smoke.

—Lynda Barry

Love is, as you know, a harrowing event.

—Anne Carson

And suddenly something unforgettable occurred: suddenly she felt a desire to go in to him and hear his voice, his words. If he spoke to her in a soft, deep voice, her soul would take courage and rise to the surface of her body, and she would burst out crying.

—Milan Kundera, *The Unbearable Lightness of Being*

Too much of a good thing can be wonderful.

—Mae West

Love is scary, isn't it? I'm not scared about commitment—that's nothing. I'm scared about love. Loving something—anything—intensely, there's major fear and awe. I guess if I were a highly evolved being I'd say fear has nothing to do with it, but I don't think I've reached that level of consciousness.

—Madonna

[I am] over the moon! . . . We are both over the moon and will be even more so when this is over.

—Prince Andrew, Duke of York,
on his engagement to Sarah Ferguson

You call it madness, but I call it love.

—Don Byas

OLYMPIA DUKAKIS: Do you love him, Loretta?
CHER: No.
OLYMPIA DUKAKIS: Good. When you love 'em, they drive you crazy; they know they can.

—*Moonstruck*

Our love is so furious that we burn each other out.

—Richard Burton, after his second divorce
from Elizabeth Taylor

It was the year they fell into devastating love. Neither one could do anything except think about the other, dream about the other, and wait for letters with the same impatience they felt when they answered them.

—Gabriel García Márquez

Head Over Heels

My soul thirsteth for thee, my flesh longeth for thee in a dry and thirsty land, where no water is.

—Psalm 63:1

My love was so hot as mighty nigh to burst my boilers.

—David Crockett,
Narrative of the Life of Colonel Crockett

Great God!—what delusion has come over me? What sweet madness has seized me? . . . Oh! I *cannot* see, but I must feel, or my heart will stop and my brain burst. Whatever—whoever you are—be perceptible to the touch or I cannot live!

—Edward Rochester in *Jane Eyre*,
by Charlotte Brontë

It was the kind of desperate, headlong, adolescent calf love that he should have experienced years ago and got over.

—Agatha Christie,
Remembered Death

When you fall in love, change sweeps through you on wings and you cannot help but lose your grip on that cherished entity, your self.

—Anne Carson

It is too rash, too unadvis'd, too
    sudden;
Too like the lightning, which doth
    cease to be
Ere one can say it lightens.

—William Shakespeare,
Romeo and Juliet

Head Over Heels

A few days ago I thought I loved you; but since I last saw you I feel I love you a thousand times more. All the time I have known you I adore you more each day. . . . I beg you, let me see some of your faults: be less beautiful, less graceful, less kind . . .

—Napoléon Bonaparte, in a letter to Joséphine Bonaparte

It was a very spasmodic courtship, conducted mainly at long distance with a great clanking of coins in dozens of phone booths.

—Jacqueline Kennedy Onassis, about her romance with John F. Kennedy

It was first love. There's no love like that. I don't wish it on a soul. I don't hate anyone enough.

—Carol Matthau, *Among the Portuguese*

Nay, but Jack, such eyes! such eyes! so innocently wild! so bashfully irresolute! Not a glance but speaks and kindles some thought of love! Then, Jack, her cheeks! her cheeks, Jack! so deeply blushing at the insinuations of her tell-tale eyes! Then, Jack, her lips! O, Jack, lips smiling at their own discretion! and, if not smiling, more sweetly pouting—more lovely in sullenness! Then, Jack, her neck! O, Jack, Jack!

—Richard Brinsley Sheridan (1751–1816)

You know, new lovers really should have a minimum isolation period of say, six months, so as not to nauseate absolutely everyone they meet.

—Kathy Lette

Love is being stupid together.

—Paul Valéry

If only one could tell true love from false love the way one can tell mushrooms from toadstools.

—Katherine Mansfield

First love is an astounding experience and if the object happens to be totally unworthy and the love not really love at all, it makes little difference to the intensity or the pain.

—Angela Thirkell, *Cheerfulness Breaks In*

First time he kissed me, he but only kissed
The fingers of this hand wherewith I write;
And, ever since, it grew more clean and white.

—Elizabeth Barrett Browning,
Sonnets from the Portuguese

I'm glad it cannot happen twice, the fever of first love.

—Daphne du Maurier, *Rebecca*

I found myself swept from the accustomed mooring of caution. Each night I felt more completely possessed by our love, carried ever more swiftly into uncharted seas of feeling, content to let the Prince chart the course, heedless of where the voyage would end.

—Thelma Furness, about Edward VIII

Love is a snowmobile racing across the tundra and then suddenly it flips over, pinning you underneath. At night, the ice weasels come.

—Matt Groening

We don't believe in rheumatism and true love until after the first attack.

> —Marie von Ebner-Eschenbach

For love to last, you had to have illusions or have no illusions at all. But you had to stick to one or the other. It was the switching back and forth that endangered things.

> —Lorrie Moore

A guy knows he's in love when he loses interest in his car for a couple of days.

> —Tim Allen

If grass can grow through cement, love can find you at every time in your life.

> —Cher

Crazy Love

L ove. Of course, love. Flames for a year, ashes for thirty.
> —Giuseppe di Lampedusa,
> *The Leopard*

The mark of a true crush . . . is that you fall in love first and grope for reasons afterward.
> —Shana Alexander

Falling in love consists merely in uncorking the imagination and bottling the common sense.
> —Helen Rowland

Love is the strange bewilderment which overtakes one person on account of another person.

—James Thurber and E. B. White

One ought to hold on to one's heart; for if one lets it go, one soon loses control of the head too.

—Friedrich Wilhelm Nietzsche

The ultimate test of a relationship is to disagree but to hold hands.

—Alexandra Penney

When you're in a relationship, you're always surrounded by a ring of circumstances . . . joined together by a wedding ring, or in a boxing ring.

—Bob Seger

. . . love and revenge grow from the same kernel of want.

—Kaye Gibbons

With you I should love to live, with you be ready to die.

—Horace

You're obstinate, pliant, merry, morose, all at once. For me there's no living with you, or without you.

—Martial

The best part of married life is the fights. The rest is merely so-so.

—Thornton Wilder,
The Matchmaker

Crazy Love 27

After seven years of marriage, I'm sure of two things—first, never wallpaper together, and second, you'll need two bathrooms . . . both for her. The rest is a mystery, but a mystery I love to be involved in.

—Dennis Miller

You cannot be neutral in a relationship. You're either contributing to it or you're contaminating it.

—Phillip McGraw

How quickly bodies come to love each other, promise themselves to each other always, without asking permission from the mind!

—Lorrie Moore

Juliet: O! swear not by the moon, the inconstant
  moon,
That monthly changes in her circled orb,
Lest that thy love prove likewise variable.

—William Shakespeare, *Romeo and Juliet*

Love never dies of starvation, but often of indigestion.

—Anne de Lenclos

Relationship is a pervading and changing mystery
. . . brutal or lovely, the mystery waits for people
wherever they go, whatever extreme they run to.

—Eudora Welty

Love's a disease. But curable.

—Rose Macaulay

Men and women, women and men. It will
never work.

—Erica Jong

Love and War are the same thing, and stratagems
and policy are as allowable in the one as in
the other.

—Miguel de Cervantes, *Don Quixote de la Mancha*

These men, it's not like we don't see them coming. Our intuition is good; the problem is we ignore it.

—Amy Hempel

There can be no peace of mind in love, since what one has obtained is never anything but a starting point for further desires.

—Marcel Proust

Love clamors far more incessantly and passionately at a closed gate than an open one!

—Marie Corelli

How sad and bad and mad it was—
But then, how it was sweet!

—Robert Browning

I can see from your utter misery, from your eagerness to misunderstand each other, and from your thoroughly bad temper, that this is the real thing.

—Peter Ustinov

Love does not begin and end the way we seem to think it does. Love is a battle, love is a war; love is a growing up.

—James Baldwin

. . . as he watched Patricia walk toward him like the shade of a nineteenth-century widow-empress in her dark gown with the glitter of all those diamonds shooting fire at her neck . . . Horacio Fortunato caught a whiff of her perfume and the full impact of her aquiline profile and completely forgot the diva, the bodyguards, his business affairs, everything that interested him in life . . .

—Isabel Allende, "Gift for a Sweetheart"

I can forget my very existence in a deep kiss of you.

—Byron Caldwell Smith

'Tis the pest
Of love, that fairest joys give most unrest.

—John Keats, *Endymion*

"You were so sweet and innocent and out of your mind," Lincoln said. "You should have seen yourself, Dot. You were quite a sight. I said to myself: This woman is either frantic, or cuckoo, or she is actually falling in love with me. Each time after you left I would drink whatever wine was left in your glass and say to myself: Am I ever going to get to kiss her?"

—Laurie Colwin, *Family Happiness*

I both love and do not love, and am mad and am
not mad.

—Anacreon

It is the same in love as in war; a fortress
that parleys is half taken.

—Marguerite de Valois

How helpless we are, like netted
birds, when we are caught
by desire!

—Belva Plain, *Evergreen*

The absolute yearning of
one human body for another
particular one and its indiffer-
ence to substitutes is one of
life's major mysteries.

—Iris Murdoch, *The Black Prince*

Crazy Love   35

If this be not love, it is madness, and then
it is pardonable.

—William Congreve

Ah, love—the walks over soft grass, the smiles over
candlelight, the arguments over just about everything else.

—Max Headroom

In love, you pay as you leave.

—Mark Twain

The course of true love never did run smooth.

—William Shakespeare

The beloved dwells at the heart of the world, and becomes a Rome: the roads of feeling all lead to him, all proceed from him. Everything that touches us seems to relate back to that center; there is no other emotional life, no place outside the universe of feeling centered on its pivotal figure.

—Mark Doty

One is very crazy when in love.

—Sigmund Freud

Love was a terrible thing. You poisoned it and
stabbed at it and knocked it down into the mud—
well down—and it got up and staggered on, bleeding
and muddy and awful.

—Jean Rhys

Sex alleviates tension. Love causes it.

—Woody Allen

Love involves a peculiar unfathomable combination
of understanding and misunderstanding.

—Diane Arbus

Love is a tyrant sparing none.

—Pierre Corneille

To love someone is to isolate him from the world, wipe out every trace of him, dispossess him of his shadow, drag him into a murderous future. It is to circle around the other like a dead star and absorb him into a black light.

—Jean Baudrillard

What we say about love and what we do about love are generally two different things.

—Rita Mae Brown

Absence makes the heart grow frantic, not fonder.

—Judith Viorst

Crazy Love   39

The Joys of Misery

There's nothing like a good heartbreak to get a good song.

—k. d. lang

I have concealed as long as I can the uneasiness the nothingness of your letters has given me. . . . If your inclination is gone I had rather never receive a letter from you than one which in lieu of comfort for your absence gives me a pain even beyond it.

—Lady Mary Wortley Montagu

Whoever has loved knows all that life contains of sorrow and of joy.

—George Sand

"In love" doesn't make one tender. It makes one furious or jealous, or miserable when it stops.

—Enid Bagnold

People have to learn sometimes not only how much the heart, but how much the head, can bear.

—Maria Mitchell

Everything we do in life is based on fear, especially love.

—Mel Brooks

A mighty pain to love it is, and 'tis a pain
that pain to miss.

—Abraham Crowley

Love is something sent from
Heaven to worry the hell out of you.

—Dolly Parton

Being in love was like running
barefoot along a street covered with
broken bottles.

—Margaret Atwood

I'm miserable if I'm not in love and,
of course, I'm miserable if I am.

—Tallulah Bankhead

The Joys of Misery

**Is love a curse or a blessing?
I sometimes think it is like
death. A strange comparison
you will say. But, like death,
it is a doorway we go
through blindfold, whether
we will or not; the band-
age falls from our eyes,
and we find ourselves in
heaven or hell.**
—Mrs. W. K. Clifford

Every little girl knows about love. It is only her capacity to suffer because of it that increases.

—Françoise Sagan

Mortal love is but the licking of honey from thorns.

—Anonymous woman at the twelfth-century court of Eleanor of Aquitaine

I have found the paradox that if I love until it hurts, then there is no hurt, but only more love.

—Daphne Rae

I wonder why love is so often equated with joy when it is everything else as well. Devastation, balm, obsession, granting and receiving excessive value, and losing it again. It is recognition, often of what you are not but might be. It scars and it heals, it is beyond pity and above law. It can seem like truth.

—Florida Scott-Maxwell

**Those who have courage to love should have
courage to suffer.**

—Anthony Trollope

**I love her and she loves me, and we hate each other
with a wild hatred born of love.**

—August Strindberg

**You see, I thought love got easier over the years
so it didn't hurt so bad when it hurt, or feel so
good when it felt good. I thought it smoothed out
and old people hardly noticed it. I thought it curled
up and died, I guess. Now I saw it rear up like a
whip and lash.**

—Louise Erdrich, *Love Medicine*

Lovers. Not a soft word, as people thought, but cruel and tearing.

—Alice Munro

Scratch a lover and find a foe.

—Dorothy Parker

The love boat has crashed against the everyday. You and I, we are quits, and there is no point in listing mutual pains, sorrows, and hurts.

—Vladimir Mayakovsky

Love and stoplights can be cruel.

—Sesame Street

Who can tell what a dark, dreary, hopeless life I have dragged on for months past? Doing nothing, expecting nothing; merging night in day; feeling but the sensation of cold when I let the fire go out, of hunger when I forgot to eat: and then a ceaseless sorrow, and, at times, a very delirium of desire to behold my Jane again. Yes: for her restoration I longed, far more than for that of my lost sight. How can it be that Jane is with me, and says she loves me?

—Edward Rochester in *Jane Eyre*, by Charlotte Brontë

One does not kill oneself for love of a woman, but because love—any love—reveals us in our nakedness, our misery, our vulnerability, our nothingness.

—Cesare Pavese

The Joys of Misery

How alike are the groans of love to those of
the dying.

—Malcolm Lowry, *Under the Volcano*

The trick is not how much pain you feel but
how much joy you feel.

—Erica Jong

Dark one, I am burned
by your harsh, mocking gaze,
then, soft as the moon, your eyes
watch my tortured heart return.

—Charles Baudelaire

Love is the only disease that makes you feel better.

—Sam Shepard

The essence of romantic love is that wonderful beginning, after which sadness and impossibility may become the rule.
—Anita Brookner

One seeks to make the loved one entirely happy, or, if that cannot be, entirely wretched.
—Jean de la Bruyère

The pain of love is the pain of being alive. It's a
perpetual wound.

—Maureen Duffy

Give me a dozen such heartbreaks, if that would
help me lose a couple of pounds.

—Colette

Who then devised the torment? Love.
Love is the unfamiliar Name
Behind the hands that wove
The intolerable shirt of flame
Which human power cannot remove.
    We only live, only suspire
    Consumed by either fire or fire.

—T. S. Eliot,
Four Quartets

Eternal passion!
Eternal pain!

—Matthew Arnold, "Philomela"

You know that when I hate you, it is because I love
you to a point of passion that unhinges my soul.

—Julie-Jeanne-Eléonore de Lespinasse
(1732–1776)

Thou art to me a delicious torment.

—Ralph Waldo Emerson

Love lights more fires than hate extinguishes.

—Ella Wheeler Wilcox, "Optimism"

We fluctuate long between love and hatred before
we can arrive at tranquility.

—Héloïse (c. 1098–1164),
in a letter to Peter Abélard

The Joys of Misery

Throwing Caution to the Wind

Love liberates
everything.

—Maya Angelou

**Of all forms of caution, caution in love is perhaps
the most fatal to true happiness.**
—Bertrand Russell, *The Conquest of Happiness*

Love forgets dignity.

—Talmud

Those who don't know how to weep with their whole heart don't know how to laugh either.

—Golda Meir

Great loves were almost always great tragedies. Perhaps it was because love was never truly great until the element of sacrifice entered into it.

—Mary Roberts Rinehart, *Dangerous Days*

Love doesn't make the world go around. Love is what makes the ride worthwhile.

—Franklin P. Jones

She was an Amazon. Her whole life was spent riding at breakneck speed towards the wilder shores of love.

—Lesley Blanch (1907–), *The Wilder Shores of Love*

Kindness and intelligence don't always deliver us from the pitfalls and traps: there are always failures of love, of will, or imagination. There is no way to take the danger out of human relationships.

—Barbara Grizzuti Harrison,
"Secrets Women Tell Each Other"

The heart is forever inexperienced.

—Henry David Thoreau

Throwing Caution to the Wind

The thing on the blind side of the heart,
On the wrong side of the door,
The green plant groweth, menacing
Almighty lovers in the Spring;
There is always a forgotten thing,
And love is not secure.

—G. K. Chesterton,
The Ballad of the White Horse

Some desire is necessary to keep
life in motion.

—Samuel Johnson

I'll come to thee by moonlight,
        though hell should bar the way.

—Alfred Noyes,
"The Highwayman"

I am mad with love. My passion is frenzy. The respect of our immediate meeting overwhelms and entrances me. I pass my nights and days in scenes of strange and fascinating rapture.

—Benjamin Disraeli, in a letter to
Mrs. Wyndham Lewis

Wild Nights—Wild Nights
Were I with thee
Wild Nights should be
Our luxury!

—Emily Dickinson

How little do they know human nature, who think they can say to passion, so far shalt thou go, and no farther!

—Sarah Scott, *The History of Cordelia*

I'll woo her as the lion woos his brides.

—John Home, *Douglas*

Throwing Caution to the Wind

To stay with you for one night I would throw away my whole life, sacrifice a hundred persons, I would burn Louveciennes, be capable of *anything*. This is not to worry you, Henry, it is just that I can't keep from saying it, that I am overflowing, desperately in love with you and I never was with anyone.

—Anaïs Nin, in a letter to Henry Miller

There's not a game in the world you can play without the risk of getting hurt some.

—Katharine Hepburn

Once begun, a love affair is like a train headed through a tunnel.

—Helen Gurley Brown

"Don't put all your eggs in one basket," is a proverb which no woman has ever yet learnt, or will ever learn, for from the beginning of time she has put all her eggs in the one frail basket of love.

—Norma Lorimer

I have no patience with women who measure and weigh their love like a country doctor dispensing capsules. If a man is worth loving at all, he is worth loving generously, even recklessly.

—Marie Dressler

I've got a heart like a college prom. Each one I dance with seems the best of all.

—Ilka Chase, *In Bed We Cry*

When first we fall in love, we feel that we know all there is to know about life. And perhaps we are right.

—Mignon McLaughlin

There is a rule in sailing where the more maneuverable ship should give way to the less maneuverable craft. I think this is sometimes a good rule to follow in human relationships as well.

—Dr. Joyce Brothers

Can love be calm, resigned, free from desire? Impetuous only a few days a year and relegated the rest of the time to a compartment in the brain?

—Louise Colet

**Whoso loves
Believes the impossible.**

—Elizabeth Barrett Browning, *Aurora Leigh*

**. . . It's so much better to desire than to have.
The moment of desire is the most extraordinary
moment. The moment of desire, when you *know*
something is going to happen—that's the most
exalting.**

—Anouk Aimée

**Relationships are like a dance, with visible energy
racing back and forth between partners.**

—Colette Dowling

**I had no use, at that moment, for wise precaution; if
wisdom interfered with love, to hell with wisdom. I
had given myself over to love.**

—Mark Doty

Throwing Caution to the Wind

You Rock My World

I couldn't sleep because I was angry thinking about him, but the fact that I was thinking about him made me even angrier, and the angrier I became the more I thought about him.

—Luisa Santiaga, mother of
Gabriel García Márquez

For the rest of the week it was all she could do to endure the terror that she might see him and the torment that she might not.

—Gabriel García Márquez

When you fall in love you abandon the forms of
ordinary life. The lover's only care is to be with his
beloved.

—Anne Carson

Your words are my food, your breath my wine. You
are everything to me.

—Sarah Bernhardt, in a letter to Victorien Sardou

Love is everything it's cracked up to be. That's why
people are so cynical about it. It really is worth
fighting for, being brave for, risking everything for.

—Erica Jong

He was the ocean and I was the sand.

—Lauryn Hill

I don't fall in love much. I mean, I fall in love every
five seconds with something, but I don't go from boy
to boy. I go from archetype to archetype.

—Tori Amos

Astounding what I feel when you are not here—
become suddenly very severe—don't care for
Eating or sleeping but filled with lovely feelings
and twice as sensitive to sounds lights colors etc.
It's all a matter of magnetic forces—Same things
that keep the Earth Circling about the sun in
constant rhythmetical waves of attraction &
repulsion making the
Complete Harmony—
Wonderful.

—Isadora Duncan, in a letter
to Gordon Craig

You Rock My World

Love comes by surprise like death. It doesn't move forward beating the *gwo-ka*. Its foot penetrates softly, softly in the loose soil of the heart.

—Maryse Condé

"I hurl myself at you," Polly said.

"It's just the other way around," said Lincoln.

"I don't know how I got this way," said Polly. "I was never like this before."

—Laurie Colwin, *Family Happiness*

He could not go on this way; always strong as an ox, his health was suffering, he slept only a few hours at a time, he was short of breath, he had heart palpitations, he felt fire in his stomach and ringing in his temples.

—Isabel Allende, "Gift for a Sweetheart"

. . . my heart beats through my entire body and is conscious only of you. I belong to you; there is really no other way of expressing it, and that is not strong enough.

—Franz Kafka, in a letter to Felice Bauer

There's plenty of fire in the coldest flint!

—Rachel Field

The moment you have in your heart this extraordinary thing called love and feel the depth, the delight, the ecstasy of it, you will discover that for you the world is transformed.

—J. Krishnamurti

I love you soulfully and bodyfully, properly and improperly, every way that a woman can be loved.

—George Bernard Shaw,
in a letter to Ellen Terry

You Rock My World

Holding her tightly in his arms and feeling her body tremble, he thought he could not endure his love.
—Milan Kundera, *The Unbearable Lightness of Being*

The story of a love is not important—what is important is that one is capable of love. It's perhaps the only glimpse we are permitted of eternity.
—Helen Hayes

Love is the irresistible desire to be irresistibly desired.
—Robert Frost

The mind I love must have wild places,
a tangled orchard where dark
damsons drop in the heavy grass, an
overgrown little wood, the chance of
a snake or two, a pool that
nobody's fathomed the depth of,
and paths threaded with flowers
planted by the mind.

—Katherine Mansfield

I am Heathcliff—he's always,
always in my mind—not as a
pleasure, any more than I am
always a pleasure to myself—
but as my own being.

—Catherine Earnshaw in
Wuthering Heights, by Emily Brontë

We love because it is the only true adventure.

—Nikki Giovanni

Anyone who's a great kisser I'm always interested in.

—Cher

When people are in love, they are in a magnetic state, and are very much astonished at themselves when they come to their senses.

—Geraldine Endsor Jewsbury

Love is not merely blind but mentally afflicted.

—Alice Thomas Ellis

How in hell can you handle love without turning your life upside down? That's what love does, it changes everything.

—Lauren Bacall

The fate of love is that it always seems too little or too much.

—Amelia E. Barr

You Rock My World

She stood barefoot in the kitchen dragging a hair-brush down through her long, black, wet Asian hair. . . . She said hello but didn't look at me. Too much engaged, tipping her head right and left, tossing the heavy black weight of hair like a shining sash. The brush swept down and ripped free until, abruptly, she quit brushing, stepped into the living room, dropped onto the couch, leaned back against the brick wall, and went totally limp. Then, from behind long black bangs, her eyes moved, looked at me. The question of what to do with my life was resolved for the next four years.

—Leonard Michaels, *Sylvia*

Love is like quicksilver in the hand. Leave the fingers open and it stays. Clutch it, and it darts away.

—Dorothy Parker

Love is so powerful, it's like unseen flowers under your feet as you walk.
—Bessie Head

It was a great holiness, a religion, as all great loves must be.
—Elsie de Wolfe, *After All*

It's no longer a burning within my veins: it's Venus entire latched onto her prey.
—Jean Racine

I have drunk of the wine of life at last, I have known the thing best worth knowing, I have been warmed through and through, never to grow quite cold again til the end.
—Edith Wharton

You Rock My World 75

Even as love crowns you so shall he crucify you.
Even as he is for your growth so is he for your
pruning.

—Kahlil Gibran

Love is many things. But more than anything it is a
disturbance of the digestive system.

—Gabriel García Márquez

A kiss may ruin a human life.

—Oscar Wilde

Love is or it ain't. Thin love ain't love at all.

—Toni Morrison

All the life of such moments lies in what doesn't show, in the buzz and sparkling wisdom—or shows not in words much but in the gaze, in the look of a face opening to another, in all the little ways we communicate the fizzy stirrings of attraction, into which both of us were falling more deeply and thoroughly as we talked and danced. An excitement, the pulse-quickening buzz of flirtation, the pleasure of discovering that talk didn't dispel the mutual attraction but deepened and strengthened it.

—Mark Doty

Love is a force. It is not a result; it is a cause. It is not a product; it produces. It is a power, like money or steam or electricity.

—Anne Morrow Lindbergh

I cannot exist without you—I am forgetful of every thing but seeing you again—my Life seems to stop there—I see no further. You have absorb'd me. I have a sensation at the present moment as though I were dissolving. . . .

—John Keats, in a letter to Fanny Brawne

Well, love is insanity.

—Marilyn French

This book was designed and
*art directed by BTD*NYC . . .

*. . . and typeset by BTD*NYC *in*
New Aster Black and Elektrix Bold.